MAKING
THE MOST OF
KITCHENS

MAKING
THE MOST OF
KITCHENS

GILLY LOVE

RIZZOLI
NEW YORK

For Judith, Charlie, Emily and Georgia and their very happy kitchen

First published in the United States of America in 1997 by
RIZZOLI INTERNATIONAL PUBLICATIONS, INC.
300 Park Avenue South, New York, NY 10010

First published in the Great Britain in 1997 by
Conran Octopus Limited
37 Shelton Street
London WC2H 9HN

Text © 1997 Gilly Love
Design and layout © 1997 Conran Octopus Limited

ISBN 0-8478-2031-9
LC 97-65577

Commissioning Editor	Denny Hemming
Project Editor	Sarah Sears
Designer	Amanda Lerwill
Picture Research	Clare Limpus
Production	Mano Mylvaganam
Illustrator	Sarah John
Editorial Assistant	Paula Hardy

Printed in Hong Kong

CONTENTS

BASIC PRINCIPLES

A kitchen should function smoothly and efficiently, but it should also be a comfortable room where you want to spend time. This is a subtle balance so the more effort you expend planning your kitchen, the less likely you are to waste energy and money trying to make a poor plan work. Be totally honest with yourself and make realistic plans that suit your lifestyle and budget, and the cooking and entertaining styles you enjoy, and you will design a kitchen you will never want to leave.

UPSTAIRS DOWNSTAIRS

Top priority in this large living space was making the most of the available natural light. A low central partition ensures not only that daylight can illuminate the entire kitchen but also that the dining and preparation spaces can successfully be divided and united at the same time. The cook can also talk to guests sitting at the table rather than working with his or her back turned. Paint colour links the two areas visually: the brick wall, the floor of the dining space, the worktops and unit plinths are all the same blue.

The room seems to exude a feeling of airiness, partly because the tiny but powerful low-voltage halogen lights which illuminate the kitchen at night appear to be suspended unaided, so delicate is the trapeze. Underlining the illusion, the thick glass shelf on the far wall is invisibly fixed and seems to float.

On a more practical note, the low wall provides effective concealment for all the necessary plumbing and electrics so the sink can be situated in the centre of the room, the stove further along the run of units, and several electric sockets fitted into the wall above the worktop. The top of the wall provides additional storage and a serving area too.

ASSESSING YOUR NEEDS

Few people undertake the project of redesigning their kitchen without some expert assistance. Investing in a new kitchen is a major financial commitment and if the project is to be transformed into a successful and painless reality, it will require a multitude of decisions that need careful thought and precise coordination. A stringent budget is sometimes a welcome restraint as it focuses the mind on what your real priorities are and saves you from buying furniture, units or equipment that are superfluous to your needs. As a rule, if you spend more than 10 per cent of a home's resale value on a new kitchen, you are unlikely ever to realize your investment. It is wise to consider, however, that a well-designed and pleasant kitchen is often a major selling point when a house is put up for sale. Equally, you

may decide to recoup some of your investment by choosing items of furniture that are unfitted or freestanding; these, of course, may be picked up and taken with you should you decide to move in the future.

Planning a new kitchen from scratch may involve the services of an architect, particularly if you are dissatisfied with the size or position of the current space. It may be that moving a kitchen from one floor to another, or from the front of the house to the rear, or taking down a wall to create a kitchen and dining space is a better solution than merely refitting an existing room. A good architect will not only tell you what is structurally possible, but will also provide sketches and drawings that will help you to visualize these alternatives. If you are planning a major reorganization of the house, the project management skills of an architect are an invaluable asset; coordinating all the different tradespeople involved, keeping to an overall budget and completing the work to schedule is a difficult task best undertaken by a professional. Even if you are redesigning an existing kitchen, an architect may suggest changing the position of a door or adding an extra window which could make a significant difference to the practicality and atmosphere of the room.

Whether you decide to employ an architect, a kitchen specialist or to do it yourself, you will have to think and plan very carefully before you start if you are to avoid irritating and often expensive mistakes that you will regret later. Kitchen specialists can transform ideas into reality but they do need a great deal of your input if they are to come up with the ideal layout.

It is absolutely not necessary to put the sink in front of a window and yet in so many kitchens that is where you will find it. In this kitchen (left) the sink has been incorporated into the peninsula unit, and in this way it is still possible to access both windows without having to stretch. And anybody washing up has the unusual bonus of being able to face the people sitting in the dining space, rather than presenting them with a back.

Although the room is divided so that the fully equipped and functional kitchen is sited at one end, this merges very comfortably and easily with the dining area. A blue-and-white colour scheme is used rigorously and effectively, from china to fabric, to create a calm but refreshing atmosphere. No other colour is permitted – apart from the neutral tones of the dining chairs, metal pans and the wrought-iron chandelier.

A well-upholstered window seat and thick cushions on the dining chairs (with practical removable covers) ensure comfort. Moreover, both chairs and window seat are exactly the right height for the table so that it is easy for the entire household to relax in front of the inconspicuously positioned television as well as enjoying family meals together.

HARD-WORKING SPACE

When space is restricted, compromises need to be carefully considered. While it is more practical in an ideal world to have a work surface between the washing zone and the cooking rings, sometimes it is just not possible.

Hard-working work areas in a limited space need durable surfaces that are easy to maintain. Here a single, seamless stainless-steel worktop incorporates the sink, stove and food preparation areas. Stainless steel can withstand any amount of heat and, as the name implies, is resistant to damaging stains caused by either acid or alkaline foods. Here it is extended over the front of the units below and in this way protects that surface from hot fat and food spills.

Powerful lighting is concealed in the extractor hood which easily covers and extends over the four gas rings, keeping the small area well ventilated. A mobile wooden chopping table with lockable castors provides an extra preparation area, while storage and hanging space is recessed behind the cooking area and open shelves are easily accessible at the end of the draining board. Slimline D-shaped handles on the unit doors and drawers are safer in a narrow galley kitchen than door knobs that may catch.

Much may be achieved by writing down exactly what it is you like and dislike about your current kitchen. For instance, many units are a uniform 90cm (35½in) high which unfairly discriminates against very tall or short people; working at such a height will be uncomfortable for them. Custom-built furniture or units with adjustable plinths can liberate the tall cook previously forced to prepare food hunched over a worktop that is too low.

The requirements of a family kitchen change as the nature of the family evolves. A family with a new baby may need to consider safety elements carefully and might choose childproof catches on cupboard doors, as well as organizing space where a young child can play under the watchful eye of a parent who is working in the kitchen. As children grow up and want to prepare their own meals, however, you will have to take into account that they may need their own space and different equipment.

Sitting down to make a comprehensive checklist of your likes, dislikes, needs and priorities is time well spent and it is worth mentioning even the smallest thing you find irritating at planning stage – however trivial it may seem. If you hate your dishwasher under the worktop, there is no reason why it cannot be positioned at waist level; and if you have a washing machine in the kitchen which seems to be incessantly in use and disturbs the pleasure of your cooking, try to find it a home somewhere else in the house.

FIRST RULES

The best way to begin planning a kitchen is to consider the position of the basic elements: the cooking equipment, the sink and the refrigerator. The formula for a convenient and safe working space between these items can take the form

PLAIN AND SIMPLE

Minimalist interiors, well executed, exude an exquisite simplicity. It is essential that all the materials are of the finest quality and every detail is perfectly constructed. Solid wood such as maple or teak matures and improves with age but needs regular oiling if these surfaces are regularly in contact with water. In this kitchen the work surface is made from a single piece of solid wood, thereby avoiding any joints where water could infiltrate. The sink is inset below the worktop for similar reasons, and sealed around the rim of the sink on the underside of the wood.

The dark richness of the natural timber is given dramatic impact by the white-painted tongue-and-groove cladding on the walls, which contrasts with the black stain that colours the cupboard and drawer fronts.

Above the worktop the simplest wooden brackets support two narrow shelves for plates, utensils and glasses that are regularly used. Yet all the joints are perfectly precise and each fixing point is virtually invisible – concealed with wooden plugs.

BEFORE YOU START

- Decide on a realistic budget that is in keeping with the value of your property, remembering to consider the potential for recouping any major investment – or lack of it.

- If starting from scratch, before you even start to plan the kitchen, decide if the existing room is in the best position. Would another room in the house make a better kitchen?

- Do you have the time or the expertise to embark on the project alone or do you need an architect or a specialist kitchen design company to supervise the installation for you?

- Make a thorough list of your likes and dislikes with reference to your current kitchen and also a list of your needs and preferences.

- Decide which layout you instinctively prefer, and then take into account the ergonomically sound principles of the 'working triangle'.

- Visit showrooms to gather ideas for overall design and appearance. Look at friends' kitchens in a new way and do not be afraid to ask if they 'work'.

- Make a portfolio of cuttings and a list of suppliers for all the elements you want – flooring, furniture, lighting. List prices and delivery times.

of one unbroken line or a closely related 'working triangle'. This work sequence needs to be confined to a distance of 5–7m (approximately 16½–23ft) and remember that you will have to include enough storage space for the materials and utensils you will use to prepare and cook food. Even if you only intend to make tea in your kitchen, you should still examine the relationship in the allotted space between the kettle, water supply, tea and sugar, cups and refrigerator. Ultimately, however, your choice of working triangle is likely to be determined by the size and shape of your current kitchen and whether or not you like that.

The in-line layout, which comprises one wall with a run of at least 3m and no more than 6m (approximately 10-19½ft), where worktops are interspersed with the sink and cooking rings, is probably the only answer for long, narrow rooms. One wall of a studio apartment would also be ideal, as you can hide the kitchen when not using it – behind hinged, fold-away doors or a long, sectioned screen.

With its design origins aboard ships, smaller yachts and aeroplanes, the galley kitchen has since been adopted in domestic interior design because it is ideally suited for small kitchens, where every inch is crucial. Counters run along two parallel walls with the sink and stove on one side, with a worktop between them, and the food preparation area and refrigerator on the other. The sequence is reasonably flexible, of course, even if the space between the elements is restricted. The corridor between the two counters needs to be approximately 1.4m (4ft) wide to provide easy access to under-counter cupboards and drawers.

An island layout is very traditional, reminiscent of huge farmhouse kitchens or the 'below-stairs' basements of grand houses, where the central table is also a serious work surface for rolling pastry, icing scores of freshly made cakes, or shelling peas by the bucketful. It is still the preferred option of many serious cooks who want lots of work surfaces. The additional central work station may even

ISLANDS & OUTCROPS

One end of this basement (far left) has been converted into a small kitchen, with the stove, all the work surfaces and two separate sinks incorporated into a peninsula unit. By positioning the sinks as single bowls on two corners of the unit, they can still be used if the hinged worktop-cum-dining shelf is raised.

If you are going to eat at the island unit on a regular basis, the work surface needs to overhang its base sufficiently to provide comfortable knee room underneath (left). Even if there is a dining table in the room, people love to congregate around the the action, a proposition made even more attractive if there is a glass or mug on the table and a stool on which to perch. An island can also provide a practical serving area, perfect for buffet-style entertaining.

Islands are best in larger rooms (facing page). Some have their own sinks for washing food, and usually groceries and implements are stored in cupboards and drawers in the base of the unit.

As a safety precaution, all island units need to be wired with power points so that small electrical gadgets, such as blenders and juicers, can be plugged in without the cords having to be trailed dangerously from the walls.

incorporate a small sink for vegetable preparation and even cooking rings, though this might necessitate an extractor hood too. It could also include a space that accommodates the more social side of the kitchen's character: everybody is always drawn – as if by magnets – to where the busy cook is working and an island kitchen is an ideal solution if your friends or family like to congregate to talk and eat together.

In L- and U-shaped layouts the working triangle works between two or three walls, an arrangement that works equally well in either a small or large room. Bear in mind, though, that however spacious your room, the triangle still needs to be contained within its optimum span. If you want to combine either alternative with a dining area,

which can often work well, you will have to position the table carefully, in order to give it a feeling of space and ease, whilst ensuring that you do not interrupt or block the working area with unnecessary obstacles.

The cooking zone

Only the cooking rings really need to be part of the working triangle; the oven or ovens and microwave may be built into a tall housing unit quite independently. An oven at eye level can be convenient for the busy cook glancing at what is cooking and it would also be safely out of the reach of young children. Wherever the cooking rings are placed, it is both safer and more practical to have heat-resistant

IN THE CORNER

L-shaped layouts are the best solutions for kitchens that also house a dining table, and in this spacious room (left) the two sides of the L-shape are fitted with work surfaces made of the same wood as the table. With no wall units and simply painted white brick walls, the interior feels more like a dining room even though it incorporates a well-planned working kitchen. There are glass-fronted drawers below the work surfaces; many cooks prefer these to cupboards as all the contents are visible as soon as the drawer is pulled out, even when it is packed to capacity.

A small L-shaped kitchen, or one where working surfaces are restricted, may need a dining table that can be used for preparing food. This table (facing page) has a durable marble top – perfect for rolling pastry, although generally too expensive to use as a work surface throughout the kitchen. Designing a layout that incorporates a variety of materials as work surfaces makes good practical sense, and this kitchen has stainless-steel worktops on one side of the vegetable sink and a solid wooden chopping block on the other.

■ 15

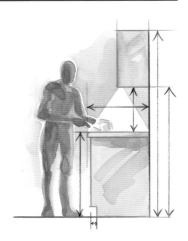

One of the major advantages of a custom-built kitchen (right and facing) over its manufactured counterpart is that all the furniture can be built at a height to suit the particular cook's most comfortable working position.

As a general rule, a work surface needs to be at hip height, so that your arms, even as you work, can be relaxed, although more strenuous tasks like rolling pastry are more comfortably undertaken at a slightly lower level. The depth of all the countertops is generally approximately 61cm (24in), as this is the standard depth of most appliances. Wall units are best hung with the bottom of the unit some 46-51cm (18-20in) above the worktop, so that the middle shelf is sitting just above eye level.

work surfaces either side. Another modern 'must' is an extractor hood above the stove. The most efficient models remove smoke and steam through a pipe vented to the outside while alternatives recycle the air above the cooking zone through a renewable charcoal filter.

The washing zone

Although the space and style of a kitchen will obviously be determining factors in your choice, a double sink is always the most practical solution because it offers you the most freedom. Dishes may be washed in one basin and rinsed in another; vegetables may be soaking on one side while you can be cleaning fish in the other bowl.

Traditionally, the sink would be positioned in front of a window. This may have been so that it could be as close as possible to the outside drain. But it would also have meant that the task of washing up – in the past probably the most time-consuming kitchen task – would at least have been sweetened by having something to look at. The recent advent and popularization of the dishwasher, however, has decreased considerably the scale of this chore so that you should no longer feel obliged to ensure a view from the sink; and if you do have natural daylight in the kitchen, you should use it instead to light the area where you are most likely to spend the greatest time. The dishwasher, meanwhile, although it should be close to the sink, can be at any level; whether you load and unload at floor or waist level is a matter of personal preference.

When you are deciding where you want to position the sink, do remember to give yourself enough storage and draining space for everyday china and utensils and cleaning materials. You might want to consider incorporating a

waste-disposal system into the sink and you will definitely need a refuse area, possibly with separate sections for cans, paper and biodegradable waste.

Washing machines have generally been accommodated in the kitchen as well, except in houses with a separate utility room or laundry, where the washing, drying, airing and ironing of clothes can be contained together. From a purely hygienic point of view, it is obviously more pleasant to keep dirty clothes away from food preparation. You may like to consider the cupboard under the stairs or even the bathroom as alternative sites as this would also free up space in the kitchen to allow you the convenience of that most liberating machine: a dishwasher.

HINTS ON PROFESSIONAL HELP

- Check out companies before you commit yourself – get references, see if you can visit some of their recently installed kitchens, and make sure you look at the quality of the materials and the standard of workmanship. Are the owners happy with the result; have they needed any after-sales service and if so, did they receive it?

- If you put a deposit on a kitchen, make sure that it would be protected if the company went out of business.

- Make sure you ask for itemized quotations for any work, materials or equipment, and check carefully to make sure that the specifications are exactly what you want.

- Be willing to be advised by an architect or kitchen design company but avoid being talked into designs either that you do not like or that you know you will not feel comfortable with, or even appliances and units that you do not need.

- Work out your own realistic time schedule and then add some more for unforeseen and unavoidable events, like incorrect measurements and late deliveries. You might be able to negotiate financial penalty clauses.

■ 17

The cooling zone

Modern technology has given us three types of cool space: the larder, the refrigerator and the freezer. Fresh foods, such as fruit and vegetables, are best kept at a cool (larder) temperature; meat and dairy products require a cooler refrigeration. The deepfreeze is used for longer-term storage of fresh and prepared foods. It is possible to buy one appliance that incorporates all three zones, so once again it is up to you – what you would prefer, or what is most suitable for the space you have available – whether you end up with the deepfreeze as a separate unit. As this appliance has to run continuously it is worth spending some time looking for an energy-efficient model; it should be well designed as well, of course, allowing you the use of every inch of space.

When you install your cooling appliances, you must remember that if they are going to be built in under a work surface, they must be adequately ventilated – either from behind or on top – to operate safely and economically.

IDEAS INTO PRACTICE

Having worked through all these practicalities in theory, you may feel confident enough to design and organize your new kitchen yourself. You may, on the other hand, feel even more in need of the expertise of a professional company; you will find that many kitchen design specialists offer a free design service, although some will charge a fee if you use the design and buy your kitchen elsewhere.

It is definitely a good idea to visit as wide a range of showrooms as possible: consciously pick up tips and ideas; start to accumulate a portfolio of designs, materials and colours which appeal to you. You should also cut pages out of brochures and magazines and start to put together a blueprint of your ideal kitchen.

Never order a kitchen from a brochure without first inspecting the showroom and examining the quality of the units and their finish. If you are unsure about a company and you do not know anyone who can personally recommend their work, make a point of asking to visit previous customers in your area. Smaller local companies are usually responsible enough to want to maintain a good reputation but it is worth checking that they can provide an efficient after-sales service. Do not be rash when it comes to settling your account either. Do not pay in full before your kitchen is installed to your satisfaction. And it is wise to check on whether your deposit is covered by an insurance scheme: you need to know that if your supplier goes out of business before your kitchen is delivered, your deposit will be fully protected.

If you are installing the kitchen yourself, make sure you can organize the electricians and plumbers to coordinate with your schedule. Bear in mind that fitting a new kitchen will probably take longer than you imagine and that it is often more convenient – and more comfortable – to work during the summer months when cooking can be reduced to a minimum. Make sure, if you are working, that the building work does not coincide with a particularly busy time in the office as it can add unwanted stress. And try to avoid clashes with important family events when you will need the full use of the room.

PLAIN PLANS

A kitchen inspired by the sea in a house which stands on a clifftop overlooking the Atlantic Ocean. Sea blues contrast with brushed metal, limestone and pale wood fitted with ring-pull handles, the streamlined appearance of these latter creating a further nautical echo.

Every aspect of the kitchen has been considered with meticulous detail. As you enter the room you are struck by a collection of fine china displayed on glass shelves in a cupboard invisibly illuminated and recessed into a wall alongside a pair of raised draining racks, next to double butler's sinks. Built into one of the adjacent cupboards is the refuse bin which can be accessed both from the front and from above – via a round lid which lies flush to the worktop. Next door again is the dishwasher and beyond that a capacious full-height double fridge–freezer. The elliptical island unit not only has a built-in fan-assisted oven and lots of storage; hidden beneath its cool metal top are gas rings, which can be used at the same time as – or as an alternative to – the Aga on the opposite side of the room. The food preparation area, with another sink and a raised glass top, stands within easy reach of both cooking appliances.

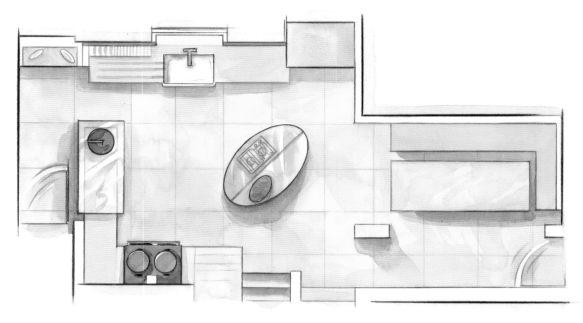

KITCHEN CHECKLIST:

What do you like about your current kitchen? What do you dislike about it? Which members of your family use the kitchen? How old are they? Is the main user right- or left-handed? Are there pets to consider? How frequently are meals prepared in your current kitchen, by whom and for how many people? Do you eat in the kitchen? If not, would you like to? Do you prefer a table or a bar? Once you have answers to these questions, you will find it easier to plan your new kitchen with a degree of focus, but this checklist will ensure that you do not forget to consider a vital element.

■ COOKING: Is electric, gas, or a combination of gas and electric your preferred option? Do you want a single or double oven, a microwave or combination oven, rings or ceramic cooktop? Will the cooker be built-in or slip-in or will it be a traditional cooker? Do you want a charcoal grill, or deep-fat fryer? Will you have an extractor fan, or filter and recycling hood?

■ KITCHEN EQUIPMENT: What equipment do you have, and what must you acquire? For cooling: refrigerator/deepfreeze, larder fridge, separate fridge and deepfreeze. For washing: single or double sink, separate extra sink, dishwasher, washing machine and tumble dryer, combined washer/drier.

■ SMALL GADGETS: Kettle, toaster, food processor, coffee maker, coffee grinder, electric can-opener – are they all essential? Plan where you will keep them before you rewire.

■ STORAGE: What can you accommodate in the available space and what must go elsewhere: china and glass, saucepans and cookware, fresh vegetables and fruit, canned and boxed food, wine and other bottles, small jars of spices and herbs, and heavy-duty objects – broom, mop or vacuum cleaner, plus the cleaning materials, and a waste bin (separated for recycling?).

■ LIGHTING: Well-lit worktops and ambience are both crucial.

STYLE

The one compliment guaranteed to make you glow with pride and satisfaction is being told that your kitchen has style! Defining exactly what having style means or how you achieve this desirable quality is open to debate; it is probably easier to define what it is not. Spending masses of money does not necessarily create a stylish kitchen, nor does slavishly adopting someone else's taste. And though you may be inspired by one look and copy aspects of many others, your own style will be totally personal.

The kitchen in this beach house in Western Australia (right) opens onto the sand and the ocean beyond. You can almost feel the warmth of the sun and the cooling breeze as it moves through the wall of louvred window doors. Comprising two island units with a hob set into one and a sink in the other, it is simply furnished; meals are probably cooked on the barbecue and eaten outside on the deck.

Echoes of the sea abound: from the bright turquoise paint which reflects the colour of the sea, to the seaweed-shaped cutouts and the furniture, which has been distressed with a wash of soft colour to resemble sea-tossed driftwood. Maintaining the natural theme, the floor is simple wood.

This country kitchen in the northern hemisphere (facing page) is cool too – like a larder – but you can imagine how warm and cosy it would be during the winter. Eau-de-nil walls and cupboards contrast with the warm tones of the scrubbed pine of the table. One wall is lined with shelves filled with rustic bowls and china, creating a traditional dresser effect, while a collection of hand-woven baskets is stored and displayed on the corridor wall outside.

COOL & COSY

The weather has a major influence on the way we live. Homes in climates that are constantly hot are constructed in a completely different manner to those that have to withstand dramatic changes from one season to another. In a country where for most of the year food is cooked on an outside barbecue and meals are eaten al fresco the kitchen design may reflect this lifestyle. It may be that ensuring that you have good ventilation to maintain a cool atmosphere inside becomes your primary concern, and of course efficient refrigeration will be vital if perishable foods are to be stored safely. Choosing lightweight furniture that can easily be moved into the garden, or onto the verandah, patio or terrace is another practical aspect to consider; it is usually made of woven cane or pale timber.

If it is continually hot outside, you may prefer to create a kitchen that will also be visually cool – by devising a pale, soothing colour scheme. Use flat matt shades of blue and grey with pale painted walls and try to avoid complicated patterns that would upset the sense of calm. It is worth remembering, however, that these decorative schemes need lots of bright clear light, or their coolness tends to become clinical and unwelcoming.

The enduring appeal of the white villages of rural southern Spain, Provence and Tuscany is due in part to the other colours – drawn from the surrounding countryside – that are combined with that white. These baked terracotta, natural sandstone and dusty pink tones also provide warmth in the winters, which are often harshly cold. Of course you can glean inspiration and decorative ideas from holidays abroad, but to transport the style of one country

to another may be completely disastrous: colours that look sensational in sunshine can feel oppressive unless you can reproduce a similar light, by natural or artificial means.

Thick wooden shutters on the windows, or canvas canopies, function not only to provide shade in summer but protection from freezing winds too. Stone or tiled floors are pleasantly cool in the summer and may be warmed up by mats or rugs if necessary. And you may have a door opening directly from the kitchen onto the garden that can be left open permanently when the weather is fine

to allow a cooling breeze to refresh the kitchen. But cool breezes become icy draughts in winter so this will probably need weatherproofing – with a warm and colourful curtain perhaps. And flexible but reliable heating that can respond quickly to changes in the weather is a modern convenience that nearly everyone would consider essential.

It is obviously sensible to wait for a year before you make any major design decisions, unless you are really confident that you can anticipate any seasonal weather changes. Real style is definitely more than surface deep.

CONTEMPORARY

While so many apparently modern kitchens are in concept deeply rooted in history, or at least have some nostalgic reference point, real contemporary style is always original. To be successful this very individual approach takes a good deal of expertise and experience and, of course, supreme confidence. These kitchen interiors are unforgiving and exacting, devoid of clutter and superfluous decoration. If necessary, in order to achieve what is considered correct proportion, form and an appropriate quality of light, rooms are dramatically restructured: ceilings are raised, windows replaced and doors moved from one wall to another.

You have to find ingenious ways to solve conventional problems, for compromise is not a word that finds space here. Colour is used dramatically and boldly; textures and surfaces are chosen for maximum impact. Everything exudes precision; every detail is completely perfect and each piece of equipment has its own carefully considered space. Whether it is constructed of natural or synthetic materials, furniture is generally custom-made.

Contemporary style suits those who enjoy clear, clean and open interiors, those for whom comfort means a room that makes them feel soothed and serene. If contemporary style were to have any connection with the past, its minimalism is most likely to have been inspired by Zen philosophy, which aims to create stillness and simplicity.

Employing an architect or designer to help you to create a unique kitchen can be a very successful collaboration; the more you involve yourself in the project the more likely it is to reflect your personality and not just be a showcase for someone else's style.

FORM AND SPACE

Major structural changes can often
create a superior kitchen. This basement
room (facing page) was made more
accessible when an extra flight of steps
was added to the original steep and
awkward staircase. These new steps
were specifically designed to provide
most of the storage required in the
kitchen. The refrigerator under the
original staircase has enough space to
allow good air circulation and a slimline
extractor hood fitted above the cooking
rings is ducted up inside the staircase.

Standard-sized kitchen furniture
would have been dwarfed in this high
ceilinged room (left). The kitchen design
here, therefore, has increased the scale
of the furniture but reduced the
complexity of each form to a minimum
of simple sculptural shapes, carefully
proportioned and dramatically lit: a
huge slab of steel spreads across a dark
blue pedestal and gleams under the row
of halogen spotlights recessed into the
ceiling; a single block of cupboards
follows the contours of the room, each
door accented by a thin stainless-steel
strip; and a row of stools – bowl-shaped
seats perched on sensually curvaceous
legs – stand in complete contrast to the
restrained geometry of the whole.

You know at a glance that this is the kitchen of a serious cook: all the plinths have been adjusted to be at the most comfortable height for its owner and it is organized with textbook precision. Following the classic L-shaped work sequence, cooking and food preparation is ergonomically contained along two walls. The cooking unit, comfortably ventilated with a large extractor hood, sits next to a small sink, followed by work surfaces before turning the corner to another larger sink with a dishwasher beneath. Each saucepan has its own place under the cooktop so that it is within easy reach when needed, while wide, shallow drawers safely store and protect the cook's knives and utensils. A narrow shelf runs all round the top of the stainless-steel splashback, a feature often found in restaurant kitchens where it would potentially be hazardous – dangerous even – if doors of upper cupboards were to be left open. This shelf houses foods and utensils that are used regularly, but it also provides visual relief from the daunting expanse of stainless steel. The remaining walls are painted in white waterproof paint, and the ceiling, with safety sensibly in mind, has been tiled with fireproof tiles.

PROFESSIONAL

While cooking and preparing food may be low on some people's list of priorities, for others these activities will completely dominate the design of the kitchen: full-time cooks and caterers may only really feel at ease in a room that has been devoted to working with food rather than dining and entertaining. Professional kitchens are planned as workplaces, taking into account the exacting regulations of commercial hygiene standards. And it is worth noting that if you will be producing food for public consumption in your kitchen, the same constraints will apply, even in what you would consider your domestic environment.

This hard-edged, industrial-looking style of kitchen may appear intimidating if you do not cook regularly for vast numbers of people, but a meticulous consideration of efficient ergonomics achieves an unexpected degree of comfort which can be very attractive. An uninterrupted run of work surfaces allows the cook to move around the kitchen at speed; in stainless steel, the preferred surface of professional cooks, it will be extremely hard-wearing and resistant to excessive heat and both acid and alkaline stains. The worktop may also include a large built-in hardwood chopping board, with a pull-out waste-disposal drawer beneath into which to scoop vegetable peelings, and perhaps a slab of cool, smooth marble as well, traditionally the best surface for rolling pastry. Otherwise a freestanding central work station with all-round access may include both cooking rings and a sink for washing fruit and vegetables. The height of all these worktops needs to be carefully calculated because at the wrong height they will make preparing and cooking food unnecessarily tiring.

Most professional cooks prefer to have access to both gas and electricity for cooking. They need bigger ovens to accommodate larger trays and baking sheets and often their stovetops have integrated charcoal barbecues, grills and griddles. Cooking on a large scale generates a huge amount of heat so an extractor hood that more than covers the gas or electric rings reduces heat and steam to maintain a pleasant working atmosphere.

Task-specific lighting is important, so that delicate jobs like filleting and icing can be undertaken without having to fight with your shadow: halogen spots provide glare-free illumination for the front of worktops and some extractor hoods incorporate a good light. Meanwhile rows of spots above the counters offer flexibility and efficiency.

Regularly used pans and utensils are always within reach – either hanging above or immediately beneath the stove. Industrial units, with adjustable shelves and frames, from which utensils may be hung, provide strong, flexible storage; they can either be fitted or freestanding. Open shelves above worktops display more equipment, which may have been chosen for its stackability, while tall, deep shelves at lower levels are used as dry food cupboards for catering-size jars, cans and more weighty items. Many cooks prefer wide drawers so all the contents are visible from above, and can be easily removed and replaced. Razor-sharp knives – a cook's most precious equipment – are carefully protected in a knife rack or felt-lined drawer.

One or even two dishwashers are essential rather than a luxury here, and they need to take a wide range of items: pots and pans as well as the standard dinner service.

UNFITTED

The idea of actually creating an unfitted kitchen is not new; recently, however, and possibly in reaction to the unbroken but rather anonymous lines of units typical of the 1960s and 1970s, the unfitted kitchen has begun to re-establish itself as more than a viable alternative – both with regard to function and aesthetics. By having kitchen furniture as opposed to built-in units you change the whole character of the space, making it more of a room than a work station.

If your aim is to create an entertaining and relaxed living area, rather than keeping cooking and dining areas more formally separated, you will find that unfitted pieces will sit more happily alongside bookcases, desks and sofas than any of their fitted counterparts – of whatever material. But unfitted furniture has other advantages too. You can take it with you should you decide to change home; just as well because a solid wood food cupboard made from quality timber will be expensive, the sort of long-term investment that you would not want to leave behind. You can also vary the height of unfitted furniture so that your work surfaces can vary in height to suit a range of functions: it is, for instance, easy to arrange for a long table with a sink and draining board built into it to be higher than one intended for chopping vegetables; or surfaces at varying levels might be incorporated into a single, movable piece.

Traditional natural materials spring to mind – natural woods with maple, teak, granite or slate work surfaces – in rooms inspired by the simple but exquisite interiors of the American Shaker communities or the vast echoing kitchens of eighteenth-century English country houses. Beautifully made work tables fitted with draining boards

and deep butler's sinks, vast larder cupboards with woven vegetable baskets on runners and built-in spice racks, and contemporary interpretations of country dressers all serve to create a traditional farmhouse feel, with all the modern appliances hidden carefully in cupboards to maintain the appropriate atmosphere. You could equally easily, however, use lacquered fibreboard, opaque or clear glass or brushed metal for a more contemporary feel.

ECCENTRIC

An interior perceived by some as eccentric in style might be deemed totally undesirable by others, and greeted with cries of horror. Some brave souls, who have a completely individual style and total confidence in their own taste, do create some stunning interiors. In these kitchens pure whim takes precedence over practicality; visual delight is often wildly self-indulgent; nothing needs to match.

Idiosyncratic kitchens are rarely formally planned; they are more likely to evolve. Furniture and furnishings are accumulated and chosen for their individual merits rather than being selected to fit into a preconceived scheme. Priceless antiques can sit happily alongside chairs retrieved from refuse tips and Japanese simplicity may be juxtaposed with Victorian gothic. The eccentric look is frequently characterized by wit and humour: someone obsessed with photography might create a kitchen resembling a dark room; somebody else might cover every available surface with scraps of broken china and glass for a mosaic effect.

True individualists have a very particular skill; they can improvise in any situation to produce original solutions that challenge accepted conventions and still 'work'. Instead of levelling and covering a scruffy and uneven concrete floor, the eccentric might varnish it – to accentuate the stains rather than concealing them. Similarly, the gleaming white surface of a refrigerator front might be considered vastly improved by several coats of vibrantly coloured spray paint.

It is not possible to copy an eccentric kitchen style because its spirit is the creation of one individual, but you can be inspired by it, admire the confidence of its creator and acknowledge that the style has a real integrity.

PURE STYLE

Very little has actually been changed in the transformation of this sorting office in Paris into a perfectly functional – if rather unconventional – kitchen. But the decision 'not to touch' is just as much a part of creating a sense of style as wiping the slate clean and filling a space with your own new formula. Style has a lot to do with recognizing the character of a place and maximizing its potential alongside, and in conjunction with, your own likes and dislikes.

The immediate attractions of this room (left) are obvious: a massive skylight floods the room with an abundance of natural daylight, and shelves, cupboards and bins that once housed letters and parcels need only the most basic adaptation to accommodate groceries and equipment.

Elaborate cooking does not seem to be a major priority in this kitchen; a real atmosphere and a wonderfully relaxed sense of space are more important. And when you are imagining pale sunny breakfasts in spring, with freshly made coffee, warm croissants and brioches, and simple romantic suppers beneath the stars and the candlelit chandelier, somehow the culinary detail does seem secondary to the atmosphere.

A TOUCH OF THE COUNTRY

In most countries, and particularly those with a temperate climate and definite winter, people naturally congregate in the kitchen, given the opportunity. Traditionally, the range meant that the country kitchen was constantly warm; nowadays its modern descendant, be it an Aga or Rayburn, an American Viking or Westinghouse, a French Bocuse or Ambassade Lacanche, appears as often in the city as in the country – a touch of nostalgia with all the benefits of modern technology ensuring a constant temperature and comfortable atmosphere which encourages relaxed meals with family and friends – a real antidote to a hectic lifestyle.

Understandably, then, country style remains hugely popular today and continues to evolve in a variety of novel contexts. Over-designed and intricately carved furniture has given way over the years to simpler designs, but the kitchen table remains an important focal point, taking centre stage in order to cater for any task, whether that be children's homework, pea-shelling, bean-slicing or bulb-potting. Whether the table is old or new it is likely to be wooden, although highly polished and valuable antiques tend not to be appropriate. Round tables are more sociable but chairs need to be a comfortable height to maximize this advantage. These do not necessarily have to be a matching set, however; a random selection of sympathetic designs can look equally effective. Upholstered cushions will give additional comfort and decorative interest, but removable, washable covers are almost essential as they will inevitably need regular washing with food constantly present. Long refectory tables, on the other hand, almost invite the use of benches – ideal for squeezing in more bodies at a feast.

Although perhaps they lend themselves less to long after-dinner chats, hard benches can hide under the table between meals, making the most of the space available.

Decoration is generally simple with natural materials tending to feature strongly. More expensive initially than other options, these not only last longer, but sustain chips and stains more gracefully, acquiring a desirable patina.

COUNTRY COUSINS

There is something about country living that appeals to everyone to a degree, wherever they may live. It may be a basic existence, particularly if the house is isolated, or if you are undertaking extensive refurbishment of a rural ruin, but the lure of uncomplicated simplicity is attractive. In this French farmhouse (facing page) the kitchen table is the result of some inspired improvisation: three planks have been glued together on breeze-block plinths. And the front of the cupboard is faced with chicken wire. Both function efficiently, and replacing the roof beams and windows was more pressing than fashionable furniture.

Many city dwellers also emulate the simple country life in their homes, be it to add a nostalgic or romantic human touch to their stressed lives or as a more self-conscious design style. The focal point of this vast, low-ceilinged room (left) is a wooden dining table in the centre of the room, while the well-tested stove–work surface–sink–work surface configuration is confined to one side of the room. Pans hang close to the cooking area, and a tiled linoleum floor is easy to maintain, hygienic, soft and warm under foot. Devoid of any really rural element, it is a room with country overtones.

FITTINGS AND FURNITURE

The best way to start to equip a kitchen from scratch is to examine your cooking preferences and then determine what is important; which pieces of equipment best suit your practical needs rather than your aesthetic aspirations. Once you have the first couple of pieces of the jigsaw fitting together, the myriad decisions involved can often have a direct bearing on each other, and others will fall into place. Start with what is vitally important and always buy the best quality you can afford.

Many serious cooks prefer one single cooking centre that combines the cooking rings and oven. The unit here (right) has four gas rings on a stovetop wide enough to include a central grill plate too – for sizzling steaks or making perfect pancakes. Pots and pans are kept warm and dry on a built-in hanging rail and in the drawers beneath the oven.

The Aga (centre), traditionally synonymous with country kitchens, is now available in a range of attractive colours and feels equally at home in the city. Agas can be electric, solid fuel, oil- or gas-fired; the standard size has two ovens with an additional warming chamber, but there is also a larger model for bigger families or for the professional catering kitchen.

An ingenious solution for making the most of a corner in a small kitchen (far right), this six-ring stove is fitted at right angles to the corner with utensils strung up on butcher's hooks on a fine rail across both walls. A chopping block on the top of a mobile unit can be slid under the worktop when not required. White ceramic tiles provide a tough and heatproof splashback behind the stove while the work surfaces on either side are of hard-wearing stainless steel.

EQUIPPING THE SPACE

Whether, having weighed up the advantages of all your options, you decide to have your kitchen redesigned or merely revamped, and once you have agreed on the layout, you will need to budget carefully for your new furniture and equipment. And while cabinets and work surfaces are obviously important, new appliances must be given priority as they can devour a large part of your available funds.

Appliances

The cooking zone is usually the most important area of the kitchen and your first big decision will be whether to combine cooking rings and oven or to separate the two appliances. Most cooks prefer a gas stove which offers fast and flexible heat; the rings may be combined with wok burners, which is practical if you enjoy cooking Chinese food. Deep-fryers or barbecue grills are other options to consider, but are only worthwhile if you are going to use them regularly. Integrating a stove into a central island unit is becoming increasingly popular as there is space on three sides to prepare food and often seating too, underlining the cooking–eating connection. If gas is not available, opt for halogen, the most responsive of the electric options.

Conversely, it is electricity that offers the best choice in oven-cooking methods. You can buy either single or double built-in ovens and a large household may require the latter, although a single oven and separate microwave might give you greater scope. A microwave is invaluable, both for defrosting, and for providing instant meals for reluctant cooks. When looking at ovens, ensure that the grill is efficient; one with a dual circuit is best so that half the grill area can be used on occasion rather than the entire roof of the oven. An eye-level grill is convenient; so too a self-cleaning facility; and good interior lighting, of course, in order to be able to check on your food's progress at a glance. You can also buy multi-function ovens, which combine a fan-assisted heat function – best for roasting meat – with a radiant heat function, which is better for baking successful pastry and cakes.

You may want to situate all the various cooking functions together and many top-of-the-line stoves today are custom-made, offering you a choice of ovens, a mixture of gas and electric rings, chargrills, griddles and hot plates. Big commercial stoves designed for professional catering kitchens are worth considering too, particularly if you are planning an unfitted kitchen, as they are freestanding. They produce more heat than most domestic stoves so they require good air circulation in the kitchen – and preferably a ducted extractor hood that covers the entire top.

If gleaming industrial steel is not your style, there are colourful enamel stoves on the market, fired by gas, electricity, oil or solid fuel, that may be more appropriate.

Particularly in keeping for a traditional or country look, this type of stove comes into its own where there is no mains gas supply, as it often generates enough heat to warm a kitchen and can usually be adapted to run a water-heating function too. Made in cast iron and designed so that heat comes from all sides of the oven, they have a reputation for turning out good bread and juicy joints of meat.

Before you set your heart on a big brute of a stove make sure that installing it will not present insurmountable problems – either because of its sheer size or its weight. And an industrial stove may not be a wise choice if you have children because the doors can get dangerously hot. Domestic models are often fitted with stay-cool systems to keep doors at a low temperature when the oven is hot.

Even if you have a dishwasher, it is worth having a double or even triple sink as well – to let you wash up, rinse and prepare food all at the same time. Large kitchens with a central island may even have space for an extra small sink specifically for food preparation. A waste-disposal unit will require a second sink, fitted with curved waste pipes to avoid blockages and a reasonable water pressure to flush away rubbish. Good-quality mixer taps will control both the temperature and flow of the water, but it is worth remembering, as you survey what is available, that simple taps of streamlined design are the easiest to keep clean, particularly if the local water produces chalky deposits, and that taps with no washers or ceramic discs will avoid a limescale build-up if the water is hard.

CLEAN AND DRY

A seam-free solid work surface (far left) incorporates a small round sink and a draining board that has a slight gradient so that water runs down into the bowl. The chopping board has been tailor-made, chiselled to grip the edge of the sink and the side of the work surface.

Draining boards are not essential, particularly if you have a double sink and if, as here (left), the room has a dishwasher. Only the saucepans are washed by hand and these are left to drip into the sink below. The counter top which surrounds this sink has been treated with several coats of tough waterproof varnish to protect the vulnerable wood beneath.

A modern interpretation of the traditional draining rack (right): water runs off these plates and bowls straight away as they are stacked at a slight angle in the two runs of slotted shelves above the sinks. Fragile, stemmed glasses do not get smeared if they are left to drip-dry after they are washed up, and they are most safely stored hanging upside down from their bases; this arrangement acknowledges both these issues. A monobloc tap swivels over either sink and a crosshead tap provides a separate source of drinking water.

PRACTICAL ADVICE

- Separate oven and rings or combined unit? A freestanding stove can be a major feature, but dividing the cooking areas offers more flexibility.
- Consider the available energy choices – gas, electricity, oil, solid fuel – in relation to your central heating.
- If you cook regularly, a large refrigerator is essential and needs to provide chilled and cold storage.
- Summer gluts of home-grown garden produce will require a large freezer.
- Invest in good work surfaces and get them fitted properly – no dirt traps.
- Every kitchen chore may be made a pleasure if you can access the relevant equipment comfortably.
- Cabinets and work surfaces should be at a comfortable height. Standard units are often adjustable, custom-made furniture is made to measure.
- Doors may be hinged on either side; merely rehanging a door may make more and better use of your space.
- Dimmers give you flexibility, changing lighting levels at the flick of a switch.
- Keep dangerous implements out of reach of young children and put childproof locks on lower cupboards.
- A fire extinguisher, fire blanket and smoke alarm are essentials.

ALL PRESENT AND CORRECT

A narrow corridor has been transformed here (right), becoming a wall of well-organized storage. Glasses and tea and coffee pots that are regularly used are displayed on different shelves according to type, style and height, all within easy reach. Maturing preserves which do not need to be accessible fill the highest shelves, while decanters and spirits live lower down. Right at the bottom, in the coolest and darkest place near the floor, is the wine, laid horizontal to keep the corks in contact with their contents.

A washing zone, confined here to a tiny alcove (right below) is lined with panels of stainless-steel mesh. The many shiny pans and lids are hung from their handles on butcher's hooks suspended from a steel bar fixed between the walls. Below them a regiment of utensils hang on a metal rack fixed to the back wall. Table cutlery is kept safe and well organized in two metal baskets above the sink. Part of the charm of this display is the bright lighting above, which emphasizes the gleaming, absolutely grease-spotless metal – grimy varieties need not apply!

Professional cooks definitely favour industrial-quality, stainless-steel sinks while big white Belfast sinks seem to be compulsory in a traditional kitchen – along with a grooved wooden drainer. There are, however, some good-quality acrylic materials available that can be cut and carved, and joined with seams that are hardly visible, in order actually to integrate the sink and drainer into a worktop. Cheaper enamel sinks will probably prove a false economy as they are easily chipped and scratched, and stain readily.

You may be incorporating a dishwasher in your kitchen for the first time – and with a slightly guilty conscience. This time- and labour-saving device is no longer considered a luxury, however, and generally they use less water than washing up in the sink would. If the kitchen is also to be a dining area, it is worthwhile asking to see your preferred model in operation before you buy it: do not dismiss the more expensive dishwashers too quickly for they not only use less water and detergent but tend to be less noisy too.

The cooling zone – and thus your choice of refrigerator and freezer – has recently become more sophisticated, in part because of the development of chilled, ready-made food as well as the frozen alternatives, and in part because of the modern trend for more fresh food, especially fruit and vegetables. Sauces and jams which were previously kept in cupboards once open now have to be kept chilled because they contain fewer preservatives than before. Many refrigerators contain one 0°C (32°F) section for fresh meat, fish and chilled foods, and another at 2°C (36°F) to keep fresh fruit and vegetables in optimum condition.

Big refrigerators do not have to be hidden away behind cabinet doors any more; they are now available in beautiful colours and even, for the organized and tidy-minded, with

SITTING PRETTY

Some storage solutions just cannot be improved upon, so while this well-established kitchen has undergone numerous colour changes over the years, the fundamental design is timeless. White walls and ceramic tiles contrast with the black marble splashback and work surface, creating a background where the shelves and doors may be painted in any colour – an economical alternative to an entire refit of the kitchen when you feel you need a change. The narrow and shallow shelving displays china and glass that has been arranged according to how frequently it is used. Mismatched items and irregular shapes (greedy for shelf space) are hung from hooks on a rail running the length of the wall – even through the bracket supporting the lowest shelf. The old and fragile jelly moulds have been tied up and hung from hoops of string.

Under the shallow sink on two open shelves are a small tin pan and some baskets. This arrangement retains an air of rustic elegance in a space that often houses floorcloths, bleach bottles and untidy collections of brushes. Storage and display have been combined in a simple, straightforward way and yet the overall impression is of sophistication.

transparent doors, making all the contents clearly visible. Virtually all refrigerators are now made CFC- and frost-free so that the nightmare of defrosting the fridge is a thing of the past. The refrigerator may be combined with a freezer, and some include an ice-maker which, if it is automatic, will need to be connected to the main water supply.

A tall and capacious fridge-freezer may well reduce your general storage requirements. And it is always better to have extra space in the refrigerator so that its contents do not have to be piled up, but rather are stored in an organized fashion – to be easily accessible. If your old fridge was too small, think in terms of double the capacity this time, and if you have limited space, consider moving your freezer to another room; it may fit neatly under the stairs, in the garage or a utility room.

Storage

A well-ventilated pantry cupboard may well be big enough to store all the food you are not keeping in the refrigerator and you will be able to see all your cooking ingredients at a glance rather than having to forage through lots of different cupboards. Similarly, a tall pull-out pantry unit makes all its contents clearly visible and gives easy, instant access. It is personal preference, however, that will have the greatest influence on whether you decide to keep all the contents of the kitchen behind closed doors or to display pots, pans, china and glass on open shelves or behind wire mesh or glass doors. One large sideboard, whether it is an inherited antique or of a contemporary design, may well provide you with everything you need, not only to display china and glass, and store cutlery and utensils, but with space for dry foods and cans too.

CLOSED DOORS

'A place for everything and everything in its place' seems to have been taken to an extreme in this kitchen (facing page): tiny cube-shaped cupboards arranged in a perfect square appear suspended on a checked pattern of white and cream ceramic tiles. One cupboard holds plates, another stores cutlery, a third is filled with glasses and the fourth is packed with cups and saucers.

In a small kitchen where countertops are limited (right), pull-out units provide extra working surfaces for preparing food. Whereas some such units have only restricted movement – forward and back from their 'built-in' positions – both these trolleys are completely movable; having been positioned where they are required, they are then stabilized by locking brakes on their front wheels. They are topped by thick solid wood chopping boards – ideal as it is easier to chop vegetables on a slightly lower-than-average surface.

White paint and tiles have been used very effectively in this kitchen, with its sloping roof (far right), to raise the height of the ceiling – visually at least. Wall units have been specially made to follow the contours of the room to make the best use of the corner space.

Mixing open shelving with worktops of varying heights – with giant drawers or pull-out wicker vegetable baskets – helps to create an informal atmosphere in keeping with the nature of a friendly kitchen where you would want to spend your time; the regimented uniformity of long runs of anonymous cupboards on the walls and under worktops tends to work in direct opposition to this, and looks a little dated today as well. Unfitted kitchens with freestanding fixtures and furniture have recently become increasingly popular, in part because they allow you gradually to create just such a personal room, adding pieces one by one, from all sorts of different sources – as and when they are needed, rather than to match a design scheme's rules.

When it comes to storing both equipment and food, the golden rule is to keep everything as close as possible to where it is most logically used. And if you don't use it, you don't need it in front of you: the space that the unwanted electric deep-fat fryer occupies might be better given over to a juice extractor, for example. Small electrical appliances should be kept on a worktop next to an electrical outlet, or above or beneath it for easy access and replacement. Mugs and beverages need to be kept wherever the kettle stands; regularly used pots and pans should be stored in wide drawers close to or underneath the stove; spices and herbs, best kept in the dark, should live in cupboards or drawers close to the main food preparation areas.

Central islands may be fitted with a canopy extractor that might itself incorporate shelves for the seasonings you use all the time, and hanging rails perhaps, for utensils and pans. Commercial kitchens tend to have all the pots and other cooking equipment clearly laid out on shelves and dangling from rails to aid the professional chef's furiously fast manufacture of food; but while masses of pans and utensils can make an attractive display, in the kitchen of the infrequent cook they may just become irritating dust traps.

Paying attention to small details can make a huge difference to the smooth running of a kitchen. Having sections in a drawer logically separates different types of cutlery and utensils, for example; choosing pans and china that stack easily will save cupboard space; fitting a wall-mounted magnetic rack or cutting slots into the back of a worktop will keep your knives safely contained whilst maintaining their sharp blades; an open plate drainer over the sink minimizes drying-up time and stores the plates where they are unlikely to get chipped; and a mobile butcher's block can provide extra chopping space where you need it. Be sure that this latter has lockable castors, however, to give your extra work surface some stability.

Furniture

In between all this equipment are all the work surfaces and furniture that coordinate your kitchen's functions. You do not have to spend a fortune at this stage, as it is quite possible to recondition and redecorate units that you might at first feel should be discarded.

Establishing the correct height of a work surface to suit both the cook and the relevant task is a design detail that is often overlooked or ignored. Heavy tasks such as rolling

out pastry or kneading bread are more comfortable and less of a strain on the back if done at a lower level, whereas you need to put less weight behind making a cup of coffee. Some standard kitchen units have adjustable plinths but obviously the ultimate luxury, custom-made furniture, can be designed to 'fit' the individual.

Shelves need to be within easy reach to avoid back strain and rarely used items may be stored even higher up; but do make sure that you have a sturdy pair of steps to hand for when you do need to access them.

Make sure that your choice of seating is appropriate. High stools are fine for quick meals or for a drink while the cook is preparing a meal but they really do need some sort of back support if they are to be your main seating. You must remember to give yourself sufficient leg room too,

LIGHT FOR A REASON

The lighting system you choose for your kitchen may have to be multi-functional, comprising well-lit work stations and a friendly, atmospheric eating area. You will have to analyse your needs and preferences very carefully before you start, remembering to take into account the variation between daylight and after dark, because you will probably want to conceal wiring where possible.

This charcoal grey kitchen (far left) could have felt cold and unwelcoming were it not for the accents of shiny stainless steel which reflect both the natural light from the south-facing window and the beams of the recessed ceiling downlighters by night. Strip lighting concealed beneath the wall units and extractor hood illuminates the top of the stove and cooking area.

This combination kitchen-cum-dining room has an extraordinarily high ceiling which requires two rows of wall lights at what would be regular ceiling level to illuminate the work areas adequately. Above the dining table tungsten bulbs, shaded by translucent glass shades, direct clear pools of light onto the dining area; they hang as if floating, and, in order to prevent any glare at suppertime, they are crown-silvered.

Natural sunlight can dramatically affect the atmosphere in any room and kitchens that benefit from masses of warm daylight are a pleasure to work in and joyful places to entertain family and friends. Not only does this kitchen (above) have a south-facing window but a rooflight directly above the island unit as well, flooding the room with sunlight. Reflecting off a natural matting floor, dappled daylight reinforces the bright freshness resulting from the room's green-and-white colour scheme. At night the atmosphere is maintained by a choice of recessed downlighters in the ceiling, wall lights, an electrified chandelier and traditional candlelight.

whether at a bar or at a big table with chairs that would be comfortable for hours. The kitchen table and its chairs are often the most well-used pieces of furniture in the home and they need to be versatile enough to cope with a variety of functions. Dining is just one aspect; the kitchen table is just as likely to become a temporary desk for homework – doing and overseeing – household budgets, or hobbies.

Light and air

A well-designed kitchen is a well-lit kitchen, a sensitive combination of natural and artificial lighting offering the most effective and versatile answer. Food preparation areas need plenty of light – daylight when possible, but artificial at night. A sink near a window, for instance, will probably need an electric light as well to make chores like washing up as painless as possible. And strip lights hidden under wall units illuminate worktops without an eye-tiring glare.

Recessed downlighters provide unobtrusive general lighting and those fitted with eyeball mechanisms may be rotated for more focused lighting – either over a work surface or to display shelves filled with precious china or glass. To create more subdued, atmospheric lighting, you could hang a chandelier of aromatic beeswax candles over the table, or even a light with a rise-and-fall mechanism, especially if you can black out the functional part of the kitchen. As well as being economical, dimmer controls can be very useful too in this respect. Remember that to skimp on lighting is a false economy: lights can always be turned off, but it is more than irritating to work in semi-darkness.

If you are to create a pleasant atmosphere for both working and relaxing in the kitchen, the disposal of both cooking smells and steam, which can cause condensation,

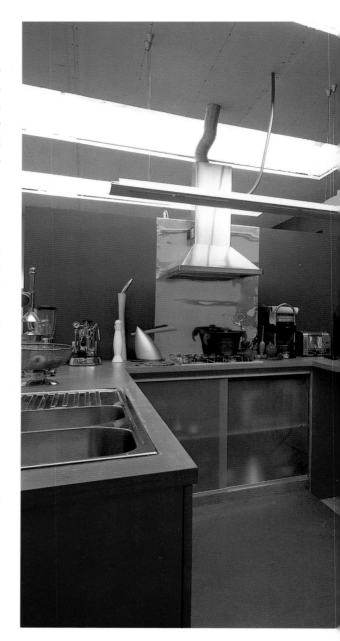

is a very important factor. Fume extractors that fit directly over the stove and which are ducted to the outside provide good ventilation. They are more efficient than those with replaceable filters. These merely re-circulate the air, though they are a perfectly adequate compromise if the stove is so sited as to make access to an outside wall impractical. Many stoves today have integral extractor hoods – with integral steam-proof lighting – which duct the cooking fumes down and away, so you may not be given a choice.

The general ambient temperature of the kitchen is an often-overlooked design detail, particularly if your plans are drawn up in the summer when the weather is warm. The most straightforward option, if space is not an issue, is to incorporate thermostatically controlled radiators at the start, on your plans. Underfloor heating, meanwhile, is as ancient as the Romans and if your new kitchen is to have a hard, cold stone or marble floor it may be worthwhile considering this. Alternatively, perimeter heating pumps out both radiant and convected heat from pipes concealed in trenches around the edge of a room or behind skirting boards, or fitted into furniture plinths. Kickspace convector heaters, which are compact and unobtrusive, fitting neatly into what would often be wasted space in the plinths of kitchen units, are an energy-efficient answer. Switch-operated, they not only provide instant heat, but may also be fitted with a cool-air option for use in hot weather.

Whatever your choice of heating and air conditioning, it is wise to invest in a system that reacts quickly. Intensive cooking generates lots of heat and a flexible and efficient heating and cooling system not only helps to keep cooking pleasurable, but allows you to sit down almost immediately to eat and relax in an appropriately refreshed environment.

LIGHT FROM THE SKY

Painting the walls of a kitchen such a deep blue takes a degree of confidence and a sensitive understanding of light and its effect on colour. These walls (left) remain lively because they are lit by three huge double-glazed rooflights, which provide continuous natural overhead lighting during the day. This illumination is replicated at night by tungsten halogen tubes which, unlike their fluorescent counterparts, give a very flattering light – almost like natural daylight – which is also restful on the eye. The stove and its surrounding work surfaces are illuminated by lights contained in the extractor hood, while the panel of sheet metal that serves to protect the wall from cooking splashes also reflects light back into the room.

If you intend to eat in the kitchen regularly, and particularly if it is also your only dining room, bear in mind that sympathetic lighting can dramatically increase the enjoyment of your meals. Natural light is most flattering for both food and faces, and at night flickering candlelight can make the simplest dish deliciously exciting.

DECORATION

The decoration of your kitchen is the one aspect of its design in which you have almost infinite freedom of choice; it is your choice of colour and texture which puts the individual stamp on a kitchen, making it completely unique. Often the decorative scheme of a kitchen, unlike any other room in a home, seems to evolve, as if naturally, as all the other elements fit together; yet with varying proportions of sensitivity and confidence you will realize your own ideas at the same time – subtle, dramatic or elegant.

COLOUR AND TEXTURE

Many people who feel relatively secure about planning the layout of a kitchen, and who find fitting all the necessary equipment into the available space a satisfying challenge, recoil at the prospect of selecting a colour scheme.

The style and look of your furniture, stove and other major appliances may influence to a large degree your decisions about colours and textures for walls, flooring and work surfaces. Once you have chosen your fixtures and fittings you may find that a colour scheme is developing naturally, or that the amount of wall space remaining is so minimal anyway that it requires no additional colour. Your crockery, glass and other visible accessories may provide sufficient additional spot colour and texture without the need to introduce any more.

WALLS OF COLOUR

A Mediterranean atmosphere has been created (left) with a bold and confident use of deep colours. Midnight blue units and cupboards contrast with a colour-washed wall. This orangey wash was inspired by the range of terracotta tones found in the floor tiles. Painted first with several coats of dark cream emulsion (latex), the wall was then painted with a fine film of thinned-down water-based burnt sienna paint which gives the final colour a luminous effect.

Paint is by far the cheapest decorating medium and, providing it is waterproof, is ideal also for sealing and colouring surfaces of wood in a kitchen. Here (right) complementary tones of soft blue and aqua green cover the panelled walls, ceiling and cupboards, chosen to match exactly the tones of the soft furnishings. The fine red line which occurs in two of the fabrics is repeated as a dado, accenting the transition from dark to light aqua on the walls.

Before committing yourself to a larger expanse of colour, you are well advised to paint a series of small test patches. The shade may look very different from your swatch and really needs to be seen *in situ* in natural light as well as under the artificial lighting of the shop.

COLOUR POINTERS

■ Large, sunny kitchens can happily
  embrace any colour scheme but
  smaller, darker rooms may need help:
  light, airy colours will tend to create
  a feeling of space.

■ Kitchens used mainly at night benefit
  from rich, darker colour schemes
  which look better artificially lit, and
  which positively glow by candlelight.

■ All surfaces need to be tough and
  hardwearing; a special paint effect
  may need the protection of extra
  coats of varnish to keep it in pristine
  condition on kitchen walls.

■ The wall space between units
  and wall cupboards needs a tough,
  durable surface of brightly coloured
  ceramic tiles, or a solid tone of
  waterproof paint, or else should be
  decorated with storage displays, such
  as gleaming knives and utensils.

■ Work surfaces may provide bands of
  horizontal colour that can contrast or
  complement kitchen furniture. They
  may vary in material and texture
  depending on their use – mix
  bleached wood with slate or gleaming
  steel with a matt acrylic composite.

Walls

You may feel that the wall space that remains may be better painted in white or a pale neutral tone to increase the size of the room, at least visually. Today, however, paint can be matched to any colour you choose, which makes it totally versatile: you can either choose to reproduce exactly the shade of another of the decorative elements of your room, or to contrast with it. Alternatively, you might feel that a country-style kitchen would benefit from a range of fresh colours that reflect the natural world – warm cream tones and butter yellow, fresh leaf greens and soft sky blues. Paint is probably the most economical decorative material too, so if you do make a mistake it is relatively cheap to correct it. It is still worth buying test cans of your shortlisted shades and painting patches on several walls – to look at the colours at various times of day and under artificial light too. Washable paint finishes are the sensible choice in the kitchen, particularly near the sink and stove.

PATTERNS & PAPER

Ceramic tiles, and particularly those with a glazed surface, are hardwearing and easy to keep clean on both walls and work surfaces. They need to be laid with meticulous accuracy to avoid leaving gaps that will attract grease and grime like magnets; handmade tiles, which can be slightly irregular in shape, are perhaps better laid by a professional.

A splashback of diagonally patterned ceramic tiles (left) picks up the blue–grey colour of the veins in the marble countertops and dining table. The same tiles are used to line the kick-space between the units and floor. The overall effect is clean and neat.

Many people avoid using wallpaper in the kitchen, but providing it has a waterproof finish, or is treated with a thin layer of clear varnish, it is still a perfectly practical option. The dado rail usefully divides this witty home-made wallpaper from a simple trompe l'oeil paint effect below that resembles a sandstone wall. The combination of the black-and-white wallpaper and the colour of the lower part of the wall is echoed and emphasized by the black wrought-iron storage unit and the naturally mellow wooden tones of the small chopping-block table.

FEET ON THE FLOOR

In any kitchen the part of the floor that needs most protection is the part immediately in front of the working areas: water and food spillages can quickly damage all but the most durable floor surfaces. Here (right) bright yellow and green ceramic floor tiles are used in conjuntion with a wooden floor. This is not only an economical solution, because tiling the entire floor in a large kitchen would be terribly expensive, but also a means of decorating an often-neglected aspect of the room, whilst avoiding an overpoweringly busy effect. The tiles protect the floor below the cabinets, while the main floor area is softer – in simple wood. Linking and dividing the two is a quasi-geometric leaf-design border. The units, meanwhile, have been painted in a paler yellow – to act as a transition between the strong tones of the floor and the harsh white-tiled walls.

You will walk and stand more in the kitchen than in any other room in the home and an old hard floor will be very tiring on the feet and legs. If you like the look of stone or ceramic tiles but not their chilling hardness, why not consider vinyl or linoleum, which have a similar appearance but are much cheaper, as well as being softer underfoot.

You may want to use a more decorative wallpaper if the kitchen is part of a dining or living room but if this is to be hung near work zones it needs to be hardwearing. If you want to use a paper that is not recommended for kitchens you can overcome the wear-and-tear problem by discreetly fitting acrylic panels over the wallpaper in any vulnerable areas – over the worktops, say. Thus, the wallpaper can be continued all around the room to create a unified scheme, whilst being protected with a wipe-clean surface in the kitchen. There are also some wallpapers available which can be painted with a protective covering but this may cause a distortion of the paper's colours.

Floors

Obviously if the rest of the home is carpeted, particularly with coir or sisal matting, it would be highly impractical to continue this surface into the kitchen. However, you can create the illusion of a large, unbroken space if you choose your floor colour carefully. You may want your kitchen floor to be a complete contrast, or you may want to introduce a a chequerboard pattern of several colours, which visually reduces a larger area.

Stone, slate and ceramic tiles will never wear out but are very unforgiving on both your legs and breakable objects. They are also very cold. This is unimportant, of course, in a hot climate and not an insurmountable problem anyway, underfloor heating or washable rugs providing potential solutions.

Solid wood floors need to be laid carefully and sealed with a tough sealant if they are to remain waterproof; chipboard or cork tiles are a cheaper option but these also need to be set on a perfectly flat surface and sealed with

FLAMBOYANT FINISH

A sweep of matt-lacquered units in deep, relaxing blue (far right) blend beautifully with shiny metal and clear glass, and provide a neutral framework for an incongruous collection of mismatched ceramics and kitchen objects.

High-quality wood has an expressive grain which mellows and improves with age; its warm tone here (right above) contrasts with sharp grey and brushed metal to create a sophisticated and truly contemporary kitchen: edges are sharp, natural and industrial textures combine, and the whole exudes clean design.

Meanwhile a traditonally designed and equipped kitchen (right below) is given a highly contemporary look: the units have simply been given a metallic veneer and finished with wonderfully quirky door handles. It is always worth remembering that it may be possible to recycle second-hand units in reasonable condition – replacing the work surface, repainting the existing doors or fitting new ones. Replacement doors of good-quality cabinets tend to be of standard size and can usually be bought off the shelf. Alternatively, have them custom-made; it will still be sustantially cheaper than a whole new run of units.

- A solid colour floor may create an illusion of more space, whereas complicated patterns will visually reduce a large expanse.
- Consider how the colour schemes from the adjoining rooms complement or deliberately contrast with the kitchen. Check that the junctions between floor surfaces are safe.
- Refresh colour schemes seasonally by changing a mat or rug on the floor, tablecloths, curtains, cushions – even pictures from summer to winter.
- Natural light is the best form of lighting – if you have it, use it to its maximum potential.
- The darker end of a kitchen may be brightened considerably by hanging a large mirror there to reflect natural light from the window.
- Very bright sunlight can heat as well as illuminate a kitchen: adjustable blinds will give you more control of both temperature and light. Beware of continuous sunshine which fades stained and solid wood furniture.
- If you enjoy constant novelty, use flowers, plants, fruit and vegetables to give splashes of instant, glorious colour that can be changed from one week to the next.

several coats of polyurethane. Working on the existing floorboards is one of the cheapest options. They will need to be sanded and then, to give a soft, muted floor colour, you can paint them with a diluted water-based emulsion paint, before protecting them with a floor sealant. Apply sealant directly onto the sanded boards for a natural look.

Linoleum is a delightfully versatile flooring material: warm and soft underfoot, water-resistant, easy to clean. Better still, it is made from natural materials. Alongside developments in technology, its physical character has been gradually improved; today it is a tough flexible surface available in a wide range of colours, and some textured looks – marble, wood, ceramic tiles – giving it huge design potential. Vinyl flooring is another cheaper option which is available in sheet and tile form. Many of the better quality designs are thicker, making them warmer underfoot and quieter to walk on – important if you have neighbours downstairs. Be sure to look for the best quality you can afford and make sure it is laid well, with invisible seams.

Surfaces that work

Horizontal colour will be provided by the work surface you choose. There is no rule that says that all your worktops need to be of the same material; it is better that they complement the units or cupboard fronts on which they sit. Inevitably, however, worktops need to be durable, and preferably heat-resistant. They also need to fit neatly, avoiding ugly gaps that can be both difficult to keep clean and even unhygienic. Granite and slate are both hard-wearing but they are expensive materials that need expert fitting for perfect joints. Marble is another natural material

PIERCED AND PRETTY

Colourwashing is really only appropriate
for large areas and works best on
kitchen walls or units. It is particularly
effective used on the panels and frames
of these cupboards (far left). The
mouldings have been defined in a
contrasting green dragged finish
and this colour is then repeated as a
wash on the drawers. And although
these cupboards here are new, this finish
gives the effect of paint that is slightly
distressed and worn with age.

Modern acrylic materials that emulate
marble or granite can be cut and carved
and joined with invisible seams so that
the worktop and walls meet perfectly
with no gaps (left). The front of the
counter is comfortably rounded; it
slightly overhangs and protects the
cupboards beneath. The soft muted grey
worktop is echoed by the window frame,
gently contrasting with the calamine
pink of the upper walls and ceiling. The
room is subsumed in a peaceful coolness.

A fine mosaic of blue and pink tiles
creates a cloudy coloured splashback
and countertop (right). To avoid an
ungainly joint, the thickness of the
counter has been determined by the size
of the tiles. Slots cut into the cupboard
doors keep the contents well ventilated.

that works well with both painted and plain wood and provides a useful cool surface. Woods such as oak, beech or elm mature and improve with age, but require sealing at regular intervals with oil or polyurethane. On the other hand, teak – used extensively in boat-building – naturally repels water, although even teak does appreciate regular oiling if it is near the sink or if you chop directly on it. There are also many acrylic surfaces available nowadays in a rainbow of colours and effects; these may be custom-made to fit the space exactly and can be shaped to form sinks, avoiding any jointing.

Ceramic tiles may be laid as work surfaces: matched to vertical splashbacks, or arranged in a decorative design between the countertop and cupboards above, or even co-ordinated with a tiled floor. Be sure that the tiles you select are recommended for work surfaces and ensure that they are laid completely flat on hardwood or a particle board surface with waterproof grouting. Even with this proviso tiles may not provide an even surface for food preparation – unlike stainless steel, which features in most professional kitchens. It is durable and easy to clean, but you will need to build in separate wooden or marble areas – or blocks – for chopping vegetables.

By far your cheapest option would be to choose from the vast range of laminates on the market, but it is certainly a false economy to buy the very cheapest; it may not be heat-resistant and if it stains and scratches easily, it will become a constant irritation. Better quality laminates, on the contrary, offer all the advantages of natural materials as well as offering you the opportunity to combine a coloured work surface – be it sober or bright, plain or patterned – with an integrated wooden chopping area.

COUNTERS OF CONVENIENCE

Accommodating both a double sink and drainer and a stovetop, fitted with a glass lid, this island unit (far left above) still maintains a feeling of space; nothing seems crowded in this compact working area. The glass lid not only helps to keep the stovetop clean; it also acts as a protective screen between the steam or spitting fat of cooking and the food being prepared on the other side of the island. Cupboards above the sink offer convenient access to essentials.

The muted tones of this blue-, green- and stone-coloured splashback and the matt green, painted cupboards (far left below) sit well with the display of opaque glass jugs and bottles above it. A solid wood worktop reinforces the natural feel that pervades the kitchen, generated by the colours of the tiles.

A narrow galley kitchen (left) has been built in the corridor that links one end of the house with the other. Natural wood, white paint and brushed steel have been juxtaposed to provide a highly sophisticated and stylish interior with overtones of café chic, but one which will also prove an efficient functional environment: easy to maintain, with everything within reach and well lit.

Picking up on details

The most cautious colour scheme can be made flamboyant if you put colourful accessories, crockery and utensils on display. If you have a kitchen table, a bright vinyl tablecloth will provide colour and protect the top. The chairs give you lots of scope too: paintwork or upholstery can be movable highlights or spots of contrast in the overall scheme.

Vases of fresh flowers or a huge jug filled with buds or branches refresh any room and temporarily alter the colour scheme. Similarly, bowls of bright red peppers or seasonal fruits can treat a monochromatic room to a burst of colour. House plants last longer and can also soften the hard edges of an interior's design. You do need to select them to suit the micro-climate available, however. And do not place plants high up on wall cupboards; they rarely receive sufficient light unless there are skylights, and are too easily forgotten. Aromatic herbs, citrus trees or fragrant jasmine all appreciate a kitchen's warmth and relative humidity: a row of herbs along the window gives you fresh natural colour and a constant source of culinary flavourings. A windowbox outside could be planted up with bulbs for a change of scenery in spring, or filled with evergreens or perennial plants to create a natural screen.

Window dressing

Maximizing the amount of sunlight in a kitchen is a vital design consideration, but you may find striking a balance between light and privacy a problem if you live very close to your neighbour. Ventilation is crucial too, so access to the window needs to be simple and safe, and you should select styles that are easy to open but which provide adequate security. You could actually increase the number of

DESIGN ACCESSORIES

A collection of antique colanders, pans and moulds (left) can make an attractive and sometimes colourful collage on a plain white wall. It is vital, however, if this idea is to be successfully replicated, that all the individual elements be kept clean and shiny. Saucepans hanging from rails must gleam too (right below) if they are to be decorative as well as merely being to hand. Here the horizontal axis of these rails is further echoed by the recipe-book holder's runner; all the little details build towards a bigger effect.

If you have a warm sunny windowsill, meanwhile, it will be ideal for growing herbs (right), such as parsley and basil, chives or chervil. Both the plants and bunches of freshly picked herbs will be a decorative bonus in any room, providing greenery, a pleasant aroma and fresher-than-fresh flavourings for your cooking.

It is not uncommon for a fashion designer to choose a different motif for each button on a jacket. Less expected here, the concept is extended with ease and style as a variety of leaf designs become handles for a flight of drawers (far right above). The darker, painted beading on each drawer not only creates a more interesting profile for the whole but consciously frames each handle too.

windows – not forgetting the massive potential of skylights – and this might prove the best investment you could make in terms of renovation. And then your window dressing must be flexible enough to address all these requirements.

Blinds are the obvious choice. Roller blinds may be fitted at the base of the window and drawn upwards to allow light from above whilst concealing the interior of the kitchen below. Café-style curtains create the same effect while Venetian blinds control the amount of light entering the room as well. And wooden shutters are a neat, clean-cut option which can add a degree of warmth.

If the kitchen is not well ventilated and the window is close to the cooking source, it is wise to choose an easy-to-clean window dressing because it will quickly be covered with a layer of grease which attracts dust and grime.

LIGHT AND SHADE

Wooden shutters may be adjusted to maximize the light in this kitchen (facing page); they can be made in sections so that the upper doors may be left open during the day while the lower ones ensure complete privacy from the street outside. At night they are completely closed and then they merge with the walls and retain the warmth in the room. While here they are painted white, they can just as easily be left as natural wood or painted a tone to contrast with the wall colour. These shutters are louvred like Venetian blinds and the fact that the sunlight can thus be filtered makes this a very attractive form of window dressing: wooden furniture, which can be quickly faded by really bright sunlight, is here given a degree of cooling shade.

A beautiful view from the sink (left above) is enhanced by four slender windows that help to provide sufficient daylight in the room; keep the kitchen cool; and, by virtue of their narrow shape, act as an important security feature in this isolated country house.

Roman blinds do not restrict the delightful view from this kitchen window (left below) but neatly fold into a wide pelmet by day and are released to just above the level of the plants at night.

SMALL KITCHENS

Preparing and cooking food in a space where everything is within easy reach and logically located is a real pleasure, and much less tiring than it would be if you had to keep walking the length of a huge room. Designing a kitchen to fit into a small space in a large room can often be a deliberate decision; perhaps the only way to stay sane as a cook in a room where entertaining and people are priorities is to contain the work area. Careful planning, however, will fit a fully functional kitchen into the tiniest room.

The famous French architect Le Corbusier once described a house as 'a machine for living'; the definition seems just as appropriate for a well-designed kitchen, particularly a small kitchen, where all the living functions seem concentrated in a limited space – from cooking, eating and even entertaining, to dish- and clothes-washing, and drying – all cogs in a well-oiled machine. This exaggeratedly high-ceilinged room has been converted into a fully-equipped kitchen without compromising any feeling of relaxed space. A floor-to-ceiling unit tucked into what would otherwise be dead space beside the window contains and conceals all the intestines of the central heating system, simultaneously creating a small but effective drying cupboard – located in an ideal spot conveniently close to the washing machine.

An extra-wide windowsill serves as a breakfast bar, which makes the most of the panoramic view from the window, while the stool that tucks neatly underneath can also be opened out into a set of sturdy steps, tall enough to provide access to the higher shelves.

INSPIRATIONS

When you are planning a small kitchen you should follow all the basic principles but you will probably end up doing more research, and having to employ more ingenuity. All this will pay massive dividends, however. Whereas in the past one-room living was usually forced upon people when their financial situation allowed nothing else, nowadays all the social stigma has gone and it is not only popular but chic, particularly in cities where space is at a premium and property expensive: from concept to execution, designs ooze practicality and efficiency.

It may be worth visiting some show flats in buildings where architects have been employed to divide up huge spaces into apartments of varying sizes; sometimes they have managed to fit the kitchens into really tiny spaces. Alternatively, you could go to a boat show and take a peek at the galleys of ocean-going cruise yachts where marine designers have designed kitchens that can cater for the appetites of a hungry crew in a situation where space is at a real premium, and where there are other considerations, such as safety, that have had to be taken into account as well. Not only may many of the general concepts be worth a second thought as the plans for your kitchen evolve, you might also come across some compact and streamlined appliances that are just what you need.

Designing for small spaces is all too often seen as problematic rather than as an exciting challenge. Yet many people deliberately choose to have a small kitchen. Those who generally eat out may decide to limit themselves to a mini-fridge and microwave, a designer toaster and the finest espresso machine, but even these few choice items

need to be accommodated with care in any design scheme if they are not to look uncomfortable. And keen cooks should take comfort from the knowledge that many of the best cooks actually prefer working in a small kitchen designed specifically for their own style of preparing and cooking food, with everything within easy reach.

For those people who enjoy entertaining but for whom the luxury of a big, social kitchen is out of the question, the idea of a self-contained working area along one side of a longer room may appeal. The first kitchen I designed for myself measured approximately 2.1 x 1.8m (7 x 6ft); a breakfast bar separated my 'kitchen' from the room proper but friends could still sit or stand and talk to me while I was cooking, and I could easily converse with people at the dining table on the other side of the room. It worked

TALL IS BEAUTIFUL

An entire wall here (left) comprises cupboards and drawers to provide ample storage capacity in this very narrow, irregularly shaped kitchen. Even access to the lockers right at the top does not pose a problem, because a metal bar has been fixed to run along the length of the wall for a simple ladder to be clipped over. For the faint-hearted, perhaps, this may look a little precarious, but, on a more practical note, it does mean that every inch of space is working hard – essential in any small room, but crucial in a work station like a kitchen.

The D-shaped handles are, in fact, more interesting than they at first appear. And it is worth noting that, ergonomically speaking, this design works better – is easier to use – if it is fixed vertically for opening doors and horizontally for pulling out drawers.

One of the drawers has been adapted to contain a small pull-out table; when not being used, it slides back and sits flush with the rest of the units.

■ 71

One alternative to the small kitchen is to combine cooking, eating and living in one open-plan space. In the 1960s, in cities like New York, former industrial buildings were transformed into single-floor apartments where all the separate elements bar the bathroom – and even that, sometimes – were designed to fall into one space. The attraction of this style of living is the luxurious feeling of open, clear and light space. Areas like the kitchen still need careful planning, and good ventilation is essential if you intend to sleep only a few feet away from where you cook. Unless you are a coffee-and-toast cook, an extractor fan or a window that can be adequately opened is advisable. In fact, even the smell of burnt toast can linger without help from a fast-acting extractor fan. This kitchen (left), positioned under one of the room's windows, is arranged in an L shape and equipped with a powerful extractor above the stove. In order to maintain an atmosphere of spaciousness, there are no wall-mounted units; the storage space has been confined to the floor, while three transparent shelves are used to display a small collection of glass and chrome.

perfectly except that there was not enough space for two people to wash up! It proved invaluable having a recycling hood, as well as an extractor fan and a window that was easily opened, as the amount of heat generated by four rings and an oven would have become unbearable in a tiny space, particularly on top of the pressure of cooking.

Sometimes drastic and bolder measures are necessary. If your kitchen space is too claustrophobic then you may want to consider taking down a wall and combining two rooms. If you do this it is worth consulting an architect to ensure that all the proposed structural changes conform with building regulations as most countries now have strict

fire-and-safety regulations as regards kitchens. If open planning does appeal, you will have to think through the ramifications of combining the functions of the kitchen and another room. Easy maintenance is crucial, for example, so that you can switch off from work mode and relax in the other half of the room without being reminded constantly about clearing up – a dishwasher may be deemed essential, so that dirty plates can disappear from sight immediately. Alternatively, the whole kitchen can be hidden behind screens or folding doors, or well-directed spotlights and low-level lamps can put the work area into virtual darkness whilst the rest of the room is illuminated.

To compromise ...

For those with a conventional lifestyle but only a small kitchen, compromises may have to be made on equipment: you may have to content yourself with two cooking rings; a single sink instead of a double; and a refrigerator with a freezing compartment rather than a freezer. There may be other multi-functional space-saving solutions that are suitable too: a double sink with a fitted chopping board as an optional extra provides a vital work surface, and similarly, some cookers (stoves) have covers or hinged lids that are flat and strong enough on which to prepare food.

Machines for both washing up and laundry are very greedy as regards space. The dishwasher must still be the greater luxury of the two and thus should go top of the hit list. And if your bathroom is small too, and cannot double up as a laundry, you will need to look for a combination washer–drier instead of two separate units.

Or not to compromise ...

Fashion consultants advise their clients to get rid of anything they have not worn for a year, and you might do well to apply the same advice in your kitchen – think of that dinner service you bought in a sale but which has not emerged from its box yet. If you cannot part with it, store it under your bed and use the space it vacates for things you do use. Similarly, the set of fish knives you are keeping for sentimental reasons, but which you always forget to use have no place in a small kitchen. Rarely used gadgets and appliances need to be given away, or swapped for others that you might use more. If you only use an electric juicer in the summer, for instance, store it somewhere else for the rest of the year, rather than wasting space.

A way of life

You may need to adapt how you shop to suit your kitchen. Nowadays shops have much longer opening hours – ideal for the small kitchen owner who can then shop daily on the way home from work. If you have been used to shopping once a fortnight, you will probably find it difficult limiting the amount of perishables you buy to the capacity of a

Conventional store-bought units may not be appropriate for odd-shaped kitchens and particularly where the available space is very restricted. You may also inherit appliances that might not appear to fit, but with some initiative you can create great things. In this kitchen a dishwasher and a place to eat have been combined in one space, a pull-out counter on a wheel being stowed away above the appliance and below the countertop proper, sliding back neatly to give access to the dishwasher beneath. The little 'breakfast table' is also useful as an additional work surface.

Historically, in a great house, the kitchen would be located 'below stairs' as a service area; in more modest houses it would probably be hidden at the back of the house on the ground floor – closer to wood or coal supplies and water. As dwelling units decrease in size, and bigger houses are converted into flats, many kitchens today are situated under the eaves. A sloping roof is unsuitable for wall units or shelving, but a series of rails can provide hanging storage for – and instant access to – mugs, cups and jugs, at the same time liberating the base units for stacking items, such as plates and bowls, or even food products.

CULINARY CORRIDOR

Even in the smallest kitchen there is usually some means of squeezing in somewhere to eat. The previous layout of this kitchen included only a rather narrow shelf beneath the window to serve as a breakfast bar. Recognizing that this was a perfect place to dine, given the view and the abundance of natural light, the new owners decided to build a platform just big enough for a table for two. Now they can sit and enjoy the garden rather than having to stand up to appreciate it. And by containing the kitchen area within four narrow partition walls, they have managed to hide the working area from sight when they are dining. These partitions also provide support for two shelves on either side of the kitchen so there is space under the worktop – even in a small kitchen – for an oven, dishwasher, and a washing machine, as well as a cupboard and drawer units. Low-voltage halogen spotlights light the shelves; much smaller than standard bulbs, these give a very concentrated beam of bright white light. And there is strip lighting concealed beneath the lower level to illuminate the work surfaces.

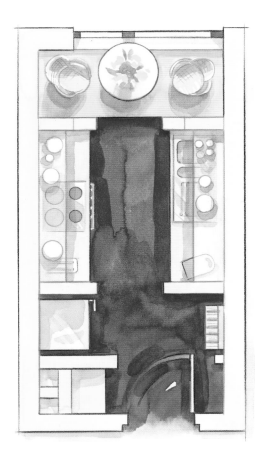

Furniture

There is always space for a pull-out counter or fold-down table and many stools and chairs fold flat to hang up when not in use. A sturdy stool with folding steps is useful too – for getting things down from high cupboards or shelves.

Custom-made furniture may be more feasible in small kitchens than in larger rooms where the cost might be prohibitive. The interiors of drawers and cupboards can be carefully designed to accommodate your crockery and gadgets. The narrow shelves that maximize space in a well-designed refrigerator can be reproduced on the inside of a cupboard door to house all your herbs and spices quite visibly in single rows. And if you have no draining board, you could install a bottomless wall cupboard fitted with a draining rack above a single sink, and store your plates wet. Large serving platters may even be better stored vertically.

A long, narrow pull-out drawer unit which starts close to the floor and runs right up as far as you can safely reach is the ideal answer for a small – often disproportionately tall – kitchen. With access on both sides, shelves at varying levels and all the contents visible, this may provide all the dry-food storage you need. And delving in the back of an untidy cupboard, where everything always gets piled on top of each other, will become a habit of the past.

Stemmed glasses are more efficiently stored hanging upside down between two pieces of dowelling than in a cupboard. And stackable china and glass, saucepans and storage containers will use less room than a mish-mash of ill-matching equipment. What is most obvious in a well-designed small kitchen is the way each item's needs have been analysed and answered, with every available inch used in the most logical way possible.

reduced-sized refrigerator, even if you are aware that you will probably be eating more healthily under this system. More economical bulk-buying of cans and dry goods may still be possible although you may only be able to store enough to hand for your immediate use; the rest will have to be consigned to somewhere less accessible. The lockers under the berths in boats are often filled not with clothes but with long-lasting food for unexpected weeks at sea.

LITTLE REMINDERS

- Conventionally sized units may be inappropriate in a very small space, whereas custom-made furniture can be designed to make the best use of every fraction of the room.

- Do not clutter precious space by keeping equipment you never use. And stacking crockery is probably better for everyday use.

- Do not scrimp on lighting. A small space may become claustrophobic if it is not well and imaginatively lit.

- Every space behind closed doors needs easy and safe access. Consider using the back of doors for narrow shelves or fixing wire racks.

- Good ventilation and an efficient heating system are vital to maintain a pleasant atmosphere all year round.

- Simple, bold decorative schemes are best; avoid over-complicated patterns or too many colours and textures.

- Small-scale equipment can often be found at specialist kitchen shops and catering suppliers. Alternatively, you might find that nautical fittings from a chandler are suitable.

- If space is tight, can you move the washing machine into the bathroom, or into a built-in cupboard in the hall, or is there room under the stairs?

Containing your kitchen in a space the
size of a wardrobe is not uncommon –
variations on the theme are found in
countless pieds-à-terre all over Paris.
Choosing to live in the centre of a major
city anywhere in the world means
compromising on space, unless you are
very wealthy. But because cafés and
restaurants are generally located close
by, it is possible to confine the kitchen
of such establishments in a tiny space;
the inhabitants can eat out whenever
they like, and so have no real need for
elaborate cooking facilities; any cooking
can be kept simple and minimal. If the
owner happens to love cooking, another
room will have to forfeit a few metres.

ALL LOCKERED UP

In this tiny apartment in the centre of Sydney one wall has been transformed into a kitchen and all but the sink and fridge–freezer have been concealed behind a series of custom-made doors and drawers. The overall impression is of a Constructivist relief sculpture, a series of white geometric shapes and shallow layers of white.

Each section has been tailor-made for the appliance or untensils that it stores. The cooking rings are contained in a drawer, the flip-down door of a cupboard storing breakfast-making equipment doubles as a work surface, with a section at exactly the right height and width for an electric blender. The same style of cupboard in reverse, with a flip-up door, held open on a locking metal arm, contains a microwave oven which can also be used to cook conventionally.

When the cook has served dinner for his/her guests, or is simply relaxing in front of the television for the evening, the kitchen can disappear discreetly behind its flush white doors.

INDEX

PUBLISHER'S ACKNOWLEDGMENTS

Conran Octopus would very much like to thank the following photographers and organizations for their permission to reproduce the photographs in this book:

1 Eric Morin; 2-3 James Mortimer/World of Interiors; 4-5 Albert Roosenburg; 6 -7 Schöner Wohnen/Camera Press; 7 Joshua Greene; 8 Alexander van Berge; 9 Richard Felber; 10 Arc Linea; 11 Pascal Chevalier/World of Interiors; 12 Mark Darley/Esto; 13 left Verne Fotografie (architect: Sluymer/Van Leeuwen); 13 right Hotze Eisma; 14 Arc Linea; 14-15 Andy Whale/Homes & Gardens/Robert Harding Picture Library; 16-21 James Mortimer(architect: Anthony Hudson); 22-3 Tim Beddow (architect: Dennis Mires)/The Interior Archive; 23 Simon Upton/Homes & Gardens/Robert Harding Picture Library; 24-25 Simon Kenny/Belle/Arcaid; 25 C. Simon Sykes (architect: Nicholas Haslam)/The Interior Archive; 26 Trevor Mein (architect: Colin Rofe)/Belle; 27 Ray Main; 29 Alexander van Berge; 30 Smallbone of Devizes; 31 Headley James; 32-3 Antoine Rozes; 34 Gilles de Chabaneix (Marie Kalt)/Marie Claire Maison; 34 -5 Nicolas Tosi (Catherine Ardouin) Marie Claire Maison; 36-7 Fritz von der Schulenberg (architect: Nico Rensch)/The Interior Archive; 37 Ray Main; 38 left Mark Darley/Esto; 38 right Henry Wilson/The Interior Archive; 39 Mark Burgin (architect: Elizabeth Watson-Brown) Belle Magazine ; 40 Trevor Richards/Country Homes & Interiors/Robert Harding Picture Library; 41 left Richard Felber; 41 right Alexander van Berge; 42 above Rodney Hyett/Elizabeth Whiting & Associates; 42 below Simon Kenny/ Belle/Arcaid; 43 Hotze Eisma; 44 Hotze Eisma/V.T. Wonen; 45 left Hotze Eisma/V.T. Wonen; 45 right Tim Beddow/The Interior Archive; 46-7 Ian Parry/Abode; 47 Dominique Vorillon(architect: T. Bosworth)/SIP; 48 left Richard Felber; 48-9 Verne Fotografie (architect: Domus); 50-1 Alexandre Bailhache (stylist: Julie Borgeaud) Marie Claire Maison; 51 Paul Ryan/International Interiors; 52 Paul Ryan/International Interiors; 53 James Merrell/Woman's Journal/Robert Harding Picture Library; 54 left Alexander van Berge; 54 right Simon McBride; 55 Mike Parsons; 56 Alexander van Berge; 57 above Otto Polman/Ariadne; 57 below Henry Wilson/The Interior Archive; 58 above Verne Fotografie (architect: Jo Crepain); 58 below Simon Brown (architect: Justin Meath-Baker)/The Interior Archive; 58-9 Tim Beddow (architect: Colin Childerley)/The Interior Archive; 60 left SpikePowell/ Elizabeth Whiting & Associates; 60 right Christian Sarramon; 61 Marie-Pierre Morel (stylist: Daniel Rozensztroch)/ Marie Claire Maison; 62 above Albert Roosenburg; 62 below Deidi von Schaewen; 62-3 Alexander van Berge; 64 Hugh Webb/Belle; 65 above left Hotze Eisma/V.T. Wonen; 65 above right Witney Cox (Designer: Charlotte Milholland); 66 Simon Kenny/Australian House & Garden; 67 above Simon McBride; 67 below Alexander van Berge; 68-9 Paul Ryan/International Interiors; 69 Otto Polman/Ariadne; 70 Nick Carter/Elizabeth Whiting & Associates; 71 Verne Fotografie (architect: Jean de Meulder); 72 Hotze Eisma/ V.T. Wonen; 74 Ralf Stradtmann/Schöner Wohnen; 75 Ophüls/ Schöner Wohnen; 67-7 left Geoff Lung/Vogue Apartments.

AUTHOR'S ACKNOWLEDGMENTS

I would like to thank everyone who has let me into their kitchens over the years – whether it be to explore or to be entertained – and Terence Conran, Malcolm Riddell, Virginia Pepper and Audrey Slaughter, who have encouraged me to write.

I would also like to thank the editorial team at Conran Octopus, who made this project possible, and in particular Sarah Sears, whose sense of humour and determined calmness has made this book a joy to write.

On a more personal note, I would also like properly to thank my parents, who have supported me, whatever I have chosen to do and whatever the consequences!